THE LAST GLACIER
AT THE END
OF THE WORLD

THE LAST GLACIER
AT THE END
OF THE WORLD

Poems

Vivian Faith Prescott

Split Rock Press
Washburn, Wisconsin
2020

ISBN 978-1-7354839-1-7

Cover photographs: Vivian Faith Prescott
Cover and layout design: Crystal S. Gibbins

Split Rock Press is dedicated to publishing eco-friendly books that explore place, environment, and the relationship between humans and the natural world. Visit us online at www.splitrockreview.org/press.

Environmental consciousness is important to us. This book is printed with chlorine-free ink and acid-free paper stock supplied by a Forest Stewardship Council certified provider. The paper stock is made from 30% post-consumer waste recycled material.

ACKNOWLEDGMENTS

My gratitude to the editors of the publications in which versions of these poems first appeared.

About Place Journal: Rewilding: "With Maps and Illustrations"; "Much Addicted to the Superstitions of Their Ancestors"

Alaska Women Speak: "Hibernacula, Hibernaculum"; "Hi-Fi"

Black Coffee and Vinyl: Ice Culture: "Die Off"; "Tongue of Open Water"

Cirque: A Literary Journal for the North Pacific Rim: "Vulnerability Assessment"

Hawaii Pacific Review: "How to Survive a Glacial Meltdown"

Prairie Schooner: "Contrary to Popular Belief"; "Top Ten Signs of Climate Change"

Rewilding: Poems for the Environment: "How to Survive a Glacial Meltdown"

Salmon Shadows, Alaska Humanities Forum: "This Prediction"; "A Snapshot of Current Beliefs"

Sheila Na Gig Online: "Indicators"; "Acclimatization"

Stirring Literary Journal: "Endangered Fifth Generation Sámi-American Displacement Due to Climate Change"

Tidal Echoes: "Frequently Asked Questions About Climate Change"

I am deeply honored to have received a Rasmuson Foundation fellowship in the literary arts and the Alaska Arts and Culture Foundation's Alaska Literary Award established by Peggy Shumaker and Joe Usibelli. These awards allow Alaskans like myself the time and means to work on our craft. I am especially grateful to my writers group, Blue Canoe Writers, and to my poet husband Howie Martindale.

To my grandchildren and great grandchildren

We had ancient methods of foretelling the weather,
now this is no longer possible.
~ Olav Mathis Eira, *Climate Witness*

TABLE OF CONTENTS

How to Survive a Glacial Meltdown   *11*

With Maps and Illustrations   *12*

Tongue of Open Water   *14*

Endangered Fifth Generation Sámi-American Displacement
  Due to Climate Change   *15*

This Prediction   *16*

Petitions from the U.S. Department of Imminent Danger's
  Field Office   *17*

Geological Forces   *19*

Indicators   *20*

Hibernacula, Hibernaculum   *21*

Vulnerability Assessment   *23*

Much Addicted to the Superstitions of Their Ancestors   *24*

Die-Off   *25*

Top Ten Signs of Climate Change   *26*

Hi-Fi   *27*

Apocalyptic Guidebook to a Glacier   *28*

Acclimatization   *30*

Frequently Asked Questions about Climate Change   *32*

How to Tell a Story Atop the Last Glacier at the End
  of the World   *33*

Contrary to Popular Belief   *34*

Meditations on Other Biological Impacts   *35*

A Snapshot of Current Beliefs   *37*

The End   *38*

The Tourist Gaze   *39*

Notes   *40*

About the Author   *41*

How to Survive a Glacial Meltdown

Acquire animal skills.
    Become a loon, a haunting crier,
swallowing the remains of this world underwater.

Learn to skin. Yourself.
    Pull your feathered hood
over your head, adjust your chinstrap

to your throat.
    Know where the sacred places are,
because there is no

safe place. Your homeland is melting
    at .25 millimeters per year.
The ocean fills your boots,

there is too much salt in your food,
    and the sandfleas are hopping
on the linoleum.

Lately, you find yourself curling
    up into the dark, nesting near
the water's edge, the place

where your dense bones
    park your truck and watch
the ocean jump the harbor's breakwater again.

What is it that has awakened in you?
    Your tremolo wavers
and the frequent hard rains

now sound like deer hooves—a clack and cry harmonic.
    You know what I mean by that—
you want to run and fly at the same time.

With Maps and Illustrations

The tourist cannot afford to lose an hour of this scenic watch.
  ~ Eliza Ruhamah Scidmore, *Appletons' Guide-book
    to Alaska and the Northwest Coast*

The Alaska route: During the excursion season
of climate change, many thousands of tourists
visited Alaska. All were delighted—charmed.

All made the same report: the matchless grandeur
of the trip, the trip of a lifetime: splendor and novelty.
There is nothing like it.

Make the usual preparations—adjust
your internal clock to the earlier plant bloom
and migration.

Spiked shoes, ice axes, and ropes are not needed—
our ancient temples are toppled; you can climb
over totems, through our old boats, and even lasso bergs.

Itinerary: A day is given to a glacier
in the tourist season. Fight a wildfire,
measure snowmelt, count dead murres.

Hike higher mountains and nightgaze
at satellites spinning faster across the sky.
Watch for sinkholes,

and make sure your immunization
for smallpox is updated—the ancient dead
are thawing all around.

Take your allergy medicines and inhalers.
We provide masks and tissues. Visit
the memorial for 125 Arctic lakes.

Photograph algae blooms. Buy vials of soil
samples of what was Shishmaref, Newtok,
and Kivalina.

Make a summer excursion to Alaska—
it is the finest and cheapest in the world.

Tongue of Open Water

In my dreams I am fully ice-covered,
    but when I awaken to warm storms

and waves, I am shredded thin.

My bed no longer hugs the coastline
    where walrus haul their bellies

across stone and ice to birth their young.

Ice now moves in later, vanishes sooner,
    and hunters travel for days and days.

What do I make of this?

They say I am an indicator of oceanic influences,
    but maybe I have convinced myself

of this importance. All I know is this condition

shows no signs of absorbing into my surface
    layer, no signs it recognizes familiar

patterns, or knows how to follow the contours

of my landscape, yet somehow fully aware
    of the age-old warning—

that I am too fragile to journey alongside

any longer; the loss of my former self,
    exposed and gaping.

Endangered Fifth Generation Sámi-American Displacement Due to Climate Change

This paper explores anthropogenic climate change influencing displacement/migration for the Sámi in Alaska.
~ Center for Global Climate Migration Research

A body will rise with the summer thaw, spring currents
will bring another to shore. There is still no trace of you

as the light falls, as shadows gather into the silhouette
of a creekbed, or appear as a log balancing on tide.

I keep glimpsing a body here and there. It's all in your
imagination, they say, this warming, this disappearing.

But this is how we will lose our next generation:
They are awakening from centuries of eroding shores.

Scattered about are flanges and teeth, a mandible perhaps.
One summer I discovered a few bones beneath

our small porch. We gave them to the high school
biology teacher for identification. He never returned them

but said they weren't human. Deer? Bear? I only know
that someone is missing the missing here and we still need

a ceremony to rid us of our cravings and the gnawing
and the scratching at the edges of what we've become—

but it's not for want of trying. Again and again,
we've tried shifting us into the shape of ourselves,

struggled to pull velvet horns over our heads,
tried enfolding into our shaggy haired coats,

and slipping our hands into claws and hooves.

At present about a dozen Sámi live on the island of Wrangell, Alaska.

This Prediction

Researchers expect that salmon productivity could shift in Southeast Alaska . . . because of climate change.
    ~ Matt Miller, KTOO Public Media

We linger in its wake, the aftermath
of brokenness, the noonday collapsed,

our animal eyes reflecting
ruin. What is to become of us?

They say we need to adapt,

that these are new conditions
and unexpected consequences.

But we flick salmon scales from our eyelids,
remember pink flesh on our tongues.

Now, I wade out to my calves in mid-winter
where nothing is a familiar universe

everything cycloid, recording this moment,
in tighter winter bands,

wondering if our circulai and the spaces
in-between speak about or don't speak about—

this warm ocean and the nearshore algae bloom,
and my magnetic field chanting their return.

Petitions from the U.S. Department of Imminent Danger's Field Office

I saved our strategic plan, held to it as it drifted
        out to sea lodged deep inside a file cabinet.

Luckily, it caught at the edge of an ice floe.

And I saved it. Saved us. They said I was a hero,
        among others. Afterward, we stood tall

under the fanfare of the new seawall,

the new paper pusher, the new claims adjuster.
        We skidded our buildings to new heights

and sites, we dried off and wrung out and hung out

in our flooded cemeteries and schoolyards.
        We slung up deer in our sheds again,

and picked fireweed blossoms from the roadside.

We said public prayers for the coalition
        between nature and the policymaker's strategic

relocation plan. We cried, oh lord I am wind-battered

and in danger of falling and rutted from rain and rain,
        eroding, rising, and sinking

into one another's arms, our souls heavy

from holding three feet of soil per year. Now,
        each morning I pray back the sea,

while my fever has risen 6.3 degrees.

But it is the end of the end of the century and our amen
        is about forgetting that a history

diffuses the lines between sea ice and the edge

of sloughing shore. All along I've known this rift
    is a sharp-toothed gaping mouth,

eating at us. And I spend every late night at the office

reading beneath our eyelids, the newest study
    for the foreseeable future

whose fine print claims you don't have to look elsewhere—

this morning it ate my grandmother's porch
    and we carried her out of her house—

her frail knees still bent in yet another prayer.

I am in charge of filing these petitions, adjusting
    the Argo floats, and counting air bubbles

in LeConte Glacier's ice. I use the ratio of heavy denial

to normal denial in ice layers to estimate the average denial
    at the moment the gray sea

claws our island's shoreface and flings it into the wind.

Geological Forces

She was covered with humankind
and their flawed gifts:

broken little birds, dried berries, their thirst.

But nothing they could offer
could make her forget the last 12.5 million years,

how the ice sheet covered the expanse,

how snow changed to firn,
then a season's melt. Over and over,

layers of corn snow melting and compressing.

She believes in her grieving,
yet believes in ordinary people,

who, like her body, will forgive the rain,
the wet earth.

But she still wonders how they figure
what to offer up to the impossible,

or if they know that all of this is holy,

especially the single snowflake crushed
beneath their feet.

Indicators

There is mention of ambient noise,
how seals hide from killer whales

among the pop and burst of a melting glacier.
There are arguments concerning how high

we live above the present sea, how our tidal days
are spent with irregular fluctuations.

Old folks comment how the winter sky
has faded into a dull blue smoke.

But all this talk weighs less than a season
of dust and who am I to question

this weeping we have awakened.
Every week I participate in a familiar rite—

rebuilding my seawall, washing sea spray
from my living room windows,

knowing there is a time-honored way
the sea has always lingered in our lungs
and rinsed out our wounds.

Hibernacula, Hibernaculum

*Bouts of torpor during hibernation usually last from a few days up
to a couple of weeks and are interjected by periods of arousal.*
~ Shannon Currie, Organization for Bat Hibernation,
Cranbrook Inst. of Science

Something like waves
caressed me awake, teeming with echoes,

although it was only a moth
tapping her wings at my window and the silver

threads of a spider's web
heavy with dew. I was simply lying motionless,

with my hand-wings enfolded
across my torpor, my breathing slowed,

tending to my body's sorrow—
this rising around me of two degrees.

How is it that overwinter
is aching so, and November's night air warms

the dandelion to flower,
and the seashore's reed grass still lingers green.

It's all about disturbance,
how seasons now embrace lavish moonlight,

and the creek beside the house
is either bone dry or bathing mossy-headed stones.

If you must intrude upon
this unsleeping, there is always room for you

beside me. Be the sound-guide
slowing my heartbeat, restoring my dreams.

Be the faint cluster
of high-pitched sounds surfing the rolling darkness

above the roof.
Be what chants me back to the bloom

of a thousand mayflies
skimming the pond, their hollow-veined wings,

ascending and falling, a current
swelling on the surface of all our urgings and ruin.

Vulnerability Assessment

Consider snow, ice, water, riparian vegetation,
fish species. For this river, with its sandtold

stories shaping the delta, engraves our island
into a scrimshawed landscape. Measure

this shift from snow to rain, early spring ice
and late snowpack, as the river ribbons

beneath my skin at a gauge height of 18 feet.
Though I've reviewed my relationship

to this river and the landforms of my graveled
driveway and my tongue-n-groove sided cabin,

it does nothing to ensure my adaptive capacity.—
For so long I have avoided questioning

the adverse impacts of my windthrown self
and my particular shallow rooting.

Much Addicted to the Superstitions
of Their Ancestors

In Sámi culture there are hundreds of words for snow.

No one else looks as closely
at the edges of light, at the wavelengths,
refracting through ancient bergs.

No one else dreams of ice as he does
at the back of the bookstore
thumbing through musty old books,

how the scent of ancient things
causes him to swoon.
This is how he finds himself

stranded on an ice-floe
every morning, sitting on the bathroom floor
staring at the small crevasses,

those shallow cuts on his skin.
They say that with the help of a seer
one can see beneath the ice.

For thousands of years he's wiped away
his same reflection—
  bođus: ice-floes floating-separately collectively;

  sáisa: mass of packed ice pressed up on or towards the shore,
from the wet mirrored glass,
an image of the light absorbing into him,

traveling deeper and deeper,
all colors disappearing until all that remains
is a shock of blue.

Die-Off

Common ice bergs washed up on the beach near our houses.
7,8000 bergs caught in the sand, wedged between drift logs,
pushed against an old floathouse.

> "I saw an eagle carry one off in it its talons."
> "I saw a tourist shove one into a satchel."

Two people on the shore clinked ice in their drinks, toasted
the end of the age.

The USGS claims there have been other die-offs,
most recently in 2000, but this is the worst they've seen.

> This is a regular part of their life history. It could be
> strong winds, or storms, maybe the ice is starving.

We are flooded with calls, wetting our feet, melting
the phones.

The official officially says it will likely turn out to be
something that has the potential

for population-level effects: It's off the charts.
They're dying en masse. They're wicked-skinny,

highly unusual disorientated bergy bits.
Biologists, geologist, glaciologist, and citizen scientist,

everyone holds dead ice

at a noticeable level—the number of carcasses,
bobbing and rolling and cracking and smacking

suggests they ingested something that is likely us.
Our toxic-analysis is pending. It's six times the normal.

Someone will present a paper at the next symposium.
Someone will say a prayer at the glacier's terminus.
Someone will roll ice across the hot skin of the Earth.

Top Ten Signs of Climate Change

1. My father tells a story of a severe winter that lingered through March: The earth shook; my cousin was swept away by a tidal wave. That winter, my father dug up a frozen sewer main by hand to unthaw it. Fishermen had a good salmon catch that year.

2. I inhale too many mosquitos now.

3. The salmon berries are rotten from the sun.

4. The thimbleberries are rotten from the torrential rain.

5. My father goes out trolling and doesn't catch a salmon. My father goes out trolling again and doesn't catch a salmon.

6. We don't eat shelled sea creatures: no crab, no cockles, no clams or geoducks. We know better.—Alexandrium species, Pseudo-nitzschia species, Dinophysis species.

7. My sister's ex sister-in-law is shot to death along with her teenage daughter and niece by my ex-husband's new girlfriend's ex-husband. He murdered them and then shot himself—and caused a heat sink scenario, the water bodies at the terminus acted as thermal energy and Shakes Glacier began to retreat.

8. My father tells the story of working in the sawmill, of working at the Forest Service, of fishing for winter kings. He stares out the window of our fishcamp, at the 50 degree ocean, and imagines another story.

9. Legend says my children's ancestors travelled over ice. My own ancestors migrated over ice across Scandinavia after the Wind Man cleared a path with a shovel. I think about this legend. I invent words for our new oral tradition: neoglacialgenic, defishification, griefologic cycle.

10. My normothermia is 101.6 degrees.

Hi-Fi

Increased ocean acidity as a result of global warming will have a negative effect on the absorption of low-frequency sounds.
    ~ U.S. researchers David G. Browning and Peter M. Scheifele

She tucks her children into the tideline,
washes their faces with sand from boulders

she has scraped for thousands of years.
Her lullaby's harsh melt lifts the night,

catches its edges on stars, until the acoustics
of seawater falls through my open window,

traveling twice as far—a hi-fi low frequency.
Her once cold rim sings to the shape-making

of sun and wind and my bay-mud footprints
walking the shore alone every night.

Her song leads me back 110 million years,
vibrates the surface of things, rattling

the water-glass on my nightstand into a tiny
whirlpool spin—the floor dust lifts up,

particles sparkle in moonlight. And, yes,
my clever hands and my exhales

are weathered in her lyrics, reminding me
the soundscape of an ancient ocean

is singing up through the fragile shell
of my own blue mussels.

Apocalyptic Guidebook to a Glacier

I trained my eyes to see,
in real time, the morning

when the gravel and ice moved back
and stumps and logs still bearing

roots and bark appeared
like storied relics,

exposed for the first time
in a thousand years.

The helicopters hovered
and boats collided

in the dazzled blink of a thousand
eyes and cameras and phones

reflecting on the ice.
What remained of its blue veins

fractured and tumbled into the bay.
The earth sprang up and we felt

a perishing groan.
Men and women in white coveralls

and white helmets
bent down with magnifying

glasses to examine
the chattermarks and striations

left as it cut away, as it melted,
as it broke off, as it surged into the inlet

And what no one considered
was the snowflea eating algae

and the bear's wet paw prints
drying in the brash light of us.

Acclimatization

She ground drifts with the wind overhead,
the first American generation Sámi Girl

A new study released

who's unable to command the wind.
She senses it there, though—

argues there is evidence that

all delicate things turn from her.
Between buildings, a deer in the alleyway

local winds are a more important factor,

lifts its head from its grazing.
Occasionally she reaches up to embrace

claiming changes in wind direction and velocity

the curl of her fear,
in the rising particles of air.

unrelated to climate change.

She is filled with lightning
and thunderheads,

Note that the wind changes consistently,

and feels ready to burst at any moment,
but into what she doesn't know.

natural variability cannot be ruled out.

She occasionally swallows a thread of wind
and it spins her around

The wind acts to change

until she doesn't know which way to go next.
Her outer garment is her too thick illusions,

        like sweat drying on the skin,

her insides tumble disharmonic.
She names these feelings,

        a pretty simple story,

these moments that shift something inside her
toward the wild.

        that's going to take people by surprise,

Call her a gradual adjustment of the body
to new climatic conditions,

        pushing it in a warming direction.

or what her ancestors named campfire sparks
in wind—spirits-blown-about.

Frequently Asked Questions About Climate Change (Before and during a tour of the last glacier at the end of the world.)

Is the ticket booth open today? If so, what are your hours?

Am I allowed to take photos?

What is the difference between climate change and global warming?

Can I record the sound of the glacier dying?

Can I bring my dog?

Do I have to wear a coat?

Do I have to bring boots?

Why is it so cold?

Is it going to be cold?

What sea level are we at?

Is there a password for the Wi-Fi?

What impact will the length of this tour have on our plans for extinction?

What impact will extinction have on our tour?

Can this melting glacier affect my allergies?

Will we get to see a real glacier in the wild?

Can I take a piece of ice home with me?

Do you mind if I light up my fossil fuels?

We are here to protect this glacier for your enjoyable experience when you come to the park.

How to Tell a Story Atop the Last Glacier at the End of the World

The ice awoke her like stars on her skin. It cast a spell and swallowed her understanding. She could do nothing but fall up into the corners of the tent, filling it with shadows. When the faded pages in her notebook and the lamplight could not contain her, she upswept through the smokehole and into the sky.

Imagine we are here on that last glacier, painting the darkness along with her, pressing our feet into a suncup, water pooling beneath all our warm palms.

There are hundreds of myths curtained with cold, glaciers that once kissed the edge of tidewater, or tongued ones spilling down valleys, others we carried in the basin of our arms.

Fortunately, we are like her, believers in legend, the power of our chants and strength of our remembering. Now, the storyteller sits on a block of ice at the edge of the crevasse where the prayers for our dead glaciers travel. We begin by tossing in our offerings: a coin, secrets on a slip of paper, a leaf, a ringed stone. And when the story arises from deep in our bellies, past our carbon-thawed throats, and into our hot-breath fog, we begin to feel even the slightest of the storyteller's words puncture through our sorrow. It flutters our scarves about our necks and lifts our skirts of blue-green light. And just like that we begin to freeze.

Contrary to Popular Belief

Daughter, our mouths have forgotten
winter—how to say it, how to feel it,

how to breathe it.
This calm disappearance

is like a traveler shedding days.
Everything has shifted beneath our feet.

We disbelieve the spring-like
grass in December is still green,

still filling ditches along the highway.
The conditions for this witness

are perfect, but aching.
We are present for our own departure.

Meditations on Other Biological Impacts

Concentration of CO_2 in the atmosphere
is now greater than any time on Earth.

They claim we are vulnerable—
our towns dotting these islands,
arching the coastline where glaciers carved
out rock faces and palm fronds pressed into mud.

Carbon dioxide absorbed by oceans.

I already know this, how our shell-bearing selves
have become fragile—
and the ocean keeps me up at night
now that my sound-dreams travel farther underwater.

When CO_2 is added to the oceans it lowers pH
causing the upper ocean to become more acidic.

All that sound—the ocean's chemistry changed,
the atoms vibrating, moving through seawater.
The glass on my nightstand
stirs up sediments.

Two and one half octaves above middle C.

In my cabin perched on the edge of the sea,
I awaken every night unable to distinguish
my own scent from a predator's. My equilibrium
chemistry measurements are no longer
anyone's concern but my own.

Cold water is more susceptible.

The oval shadow on the wall beside my bed
dissolves in seawater—merely a drum I ordered
from a catalogue. We used to sing up whales,
and cause storms to twist the waves.

Many organisms on land and in the oceans
are very sensitive to small changes in pH.

Now, I've settled in for the duration
with my delicately balanced symbiosis,
as I wait for the upwelling, the pull of water,
and for my saturation horizon to rise.

A Snapshot of Current Beliefs

I think of the sea exhaling and inhaling
          against the shoreline, forming it

into unrecognizable shapes, how the
          ocean curves beyond our line of sight.

I think of the sky chasing the sun
          into an evening blush,

and the morning winds and afternoon torrents.
          We've had months of this:

the rain washing salmon eggs from
          streams, the algae cloud beneath

the surface. I sense the ocean here
          is different—

the weight of the gods' footfalls
          sink down. Our faith has dulled,

once hook-sharp, pressed against
          our whorled thumbs.

Still, the holy ones venture out
          into the dark hush

to try and save us from ourselves.
          They practice prayers

to change these rainfall patterns,
          and quickly repair our seawalls.

But all the crows have flown
          to their roosts and only

the loons and the herons are present
          to bear witness.

The End

We buried you in our palmed hands
in earth dampened with our tears.

Grief now comes in flailing animal waves
despite having offered you the skin

of our histories to fold over us
like flags or shrouds.

The end will be simple, you once said,
something like a whisper,

like our creek splashing over stones,
a sound only the crows can hear.

The Tourist Gaze

The state of the snow appears like an old myth. Nobody's paying attention, though, to the downwasting, or to the half-starved eyes disembarking as busloads of sightseers. Some folks wander into our yards to touch our shoulders. We feel their breath on our necks before we spy their eager curious lenses; when we turn, they pretend to take photos of nearby objects. The tourists ask the same questions: Why are you mowing the lawn that isn't there? How far above sea-level are we? Do you take American money? Can I touch your moraine shoal? The ice floes have jammed up against our houses again. The frigid water pools up. In the name of the farthest sun and the ghosts of glacier fire, the travelers long to be baptized in our yards. Someone down the street has already begun this custom. The tourists pass our houses, strolling on sidewalks cracked with our isostatic uplift. Some hold small plastic bags of glacier ice, others are weeping—this scene of our dying is too much to believe. As they return to their buses they double-check their list of souvenirs: a recyclable bottle from our garbage dump, a volcano eruption, a jug of fertilizer, and the possibility of clouds.

NOTES

"With Maps and Illustrations" inspired by *Appletons' Guide-book to Alaska and the Northwest Coast* by Eliza Ruhamah Scidmore, January 1, 1899, New York: D. Appleton and Company.

"Die-Off" is inspired from "Massive Seabird Die-off Lines Whittier Beaches with Carcasses" by Zaz Hollander, Jan. 5, 2016, Alaska Dispatch News; "Murre Die-off Around Kachemak Bay Estimated to be in the Thousands" by Daysha Eaton, KBBI, Dec. 26, 2015.

"Acclimatization" borrows lines from the article "Study: Natural Changes in Wind Cause Pacific Warming" by Jeff Barnard, *KOMO News*.

"This Prediction" inspired by *Alaska Sockeye Salmon Scale Patterns as Indicators of Climatic and Ocean Shifts in the North Pacific Ocean* by Ellen C. Martinson, John H. Helle, Dennis L. Scarnecchia, and Houston. Hs. Stokes, Alaska Fisheries Science Center.

Shakes Glacier is a lake-calving glacier located 18 miles from Wrangell, Alaska up the Stikine River. The rate of terminus recession is 351 feet per year.

LeConte Glacier (Thunder Glacier) is an active advancing glacier located about 20 miles from the mouth of the Stikine River and nearby Wrangell, Alaska. In 2019 scientists discovered through acoustic observations that the submarine part of LeConte Glacier is melting faster than previously known.

Sitaantaagu, Mendenhall Glacier, is located near Juneau Alaska. Since the mid-1700s, the Mendenhall Glacier has retreated 2.5 miles.

ABOUT THE AUTHOR

Vivian Faith Prescott was born and raised in Wrangell, a small island community is Southeastern Alaska. She lives in Wrangell at her family's fishcamp—Mickey's Fishcamp. She holds an MFA from the University of Alaska and a PhD in Cross Cultural Studies from the University of Alaska Fairbanks. She's a founding member of Community Roots, the first LGBTQ group on the island. Prescott is also a member of the Pacific Sámi Searvi, and writes frequently about Sámi diaspora and climate change in Alaska. She is a two-time recipient of a Rasmuson Fellowship (2015, 2019) and a recipient of the Alaska Literary Award (2017). Prescott is the author of four chapbooks, two full-length poetry books, and a short story collection. Her work has been nominated for Pushcart Prizes and Best of the Net. Along with her daughter, Vivian Mork Yéilk', she writes a column for the *Juneau Empire* called Planet Alaska. For more information, visit: vivianfaithprescott.com. Twitter: planet_alaska and poet_tweet.